The Shakespeare Library

Julius Caesar

WENDY GREENHILL

**HEAD OF EDUCATION,
ROYAL SHAKESPEARE COMPANY**

Heinemann Library,
an imprint of Heinemann Publishers (Oxford) Ltd,
Halley Court, Jordan Hill, Oxford, England, OX2 8EJ.

OXFORD LONDON EDINBURGH MADRID PARIS
ATHENS BOLOGNA MELBOURNE SYDNEY
AUCKLAND SINGAPORE TOKYO IBADAN
NAIROBI GABORONE HARARE PORTSMOUTH NH (USA)

First published 1995
95 96 97 10 9 8 7 6 5 4 3 2 1

British Library Cataloguing in Publication Data
Greenhill, Wendy
'Julius Caesar'. – (Shakespeare Library)
I. Title II. Series
822.33

ISBN 0 431 07552 2

Designed by Green Door Design Ltd
Printed and bound in Hong Kong

Acknowledgements
The author and publishers would like to thank the following for
permission to reproduce photographs:

Angus McBean/Shakespeare Centre Library p21, 28
British Museum p9 Donald Cooper pp13, 15, 17, 22, 24, 25, 26, 29, 30
Girauden p4 Joe Cocks Studio Collection/Shakespeare Centre Library
p31 New York Public Library for the Performing Arts p20 Sonia
Halliday Photographs/FHC Burch p11 The Bridgeman Art Library p2
The Kobal Collection/MGM p27 University of Bristol Theatre
Collection p18

The cover shows a scene from the 1987 RSC production of
Julius Caesar.

Names in **bold** in the text are characters in the play.

CONTENTS

INTRODUCTION

L ondon in the 1590s was seething with activity. It was a European centre for trade and business and had expanded rapidly during the reign of Queen Elizabeth I to a population of 200,000 people.

Public entertainment had also blossomed, particularly in the area south of the Thames near London Bridge. Taverns, bear gardens, cock-fighting pits and theatres stood side by side. William Shakespeare was one of the managers of a company of actors known as the Lord Chamberlain's Men. The company attracted large audiences, was sometimes invited to perform at Court and was confident enough to be planning its own new theatre, The Globe.

Shakespeare was manager, share-holder, actor and playwright, of

A bust of Julius Caesar, believed to be the most authentic portrait of the dictator in existence.

the Lord Chamberlain's Men and as keen as anyone to do well. His new play, *Julius Caesar*, was performed at The Globe in 1599, possibly as its opening production. It was an instant success and was performed regularly from then on. Thomas Platter, a Swiss visitor to London in 1599, made this note in his diary:

'After lunch on 21 September, at about two o'clock, I and my party crossed the river, and there in the house with the thatched roof we saw an excellent performance of the tragedy of the first Emperor Julius Caesar...'

Shakespeare took advantage of the Elizabethans' enthusiasm for the history of ancient Greece and Rome. One of the best-selling books of the time was an English translation by Sir Thomas North of *Plutarch's Lives of the Noble Greeks and Romans*. It brought history to life through the personalities of the people involved. Plutarch showed **Mark Antony**, for example, not only as a great Roman soldier but also as a popular leader – a man who would have a drink and spend time with his men and who later had a scandalous love affair with Cleopatra, the Queen of Egypt.

Shakespeare and other playwrights used the portraits of characters and the account of events given by Plutarch as the source of several plays. Shakespeare continued the story of the politics and personalities of ancient Rome in a later play, *Antony and Cleopatra.*

Why were the Elizabethans so fascinated by ancient Rome? One reason seems to be that they saw parallels between the past and the present. *Julius Caesar* made them think about some of the urgent political questions of their own time, but at a safe distance. Ideas about power and power-sharing in the government of a country, the question of an heir, and the threat of rebellion against the established leader were all very real issues during Elizabeth's reign. They are at the heart of Shakespeare's play and made glamorous, for the Elizabethans, by being placed in a fashionable period of history.

In considering *Julius Caesar* today as a student or an actor we need to be aware of three periods of time:

- the moment when Shakespeare was writing the play 400 years ago in Elizabethan London
- the historical time he was writing about, 2000 years ago in Rome
- those experiences in political and public life today which connect with the play.

The Lord Chamberlain's Men had to understand the characters and events of Shakespeare's play through their own view of the problems of government in the 1590s. Similarly, a modern theatre company has to get inside the world of *Julius Caesar* through its understanding of power and the abuse of power today.

Any play performed on stage invites its audience to make connections, to allow its thoughts, feelings and experience of life to be touched directly.

An official portrait of Elizabeth I, painted in 1588.

REPUBLICAN ROME

In earlier days Rome had been ruled by kings, some of whom had been ruthless or unjust. The cruelty and overbearing pride of a King called Tarquin had been the final blow, and he was overthrown. An ancestor of Brutus played a leading part in expelling him from Rome and in establishing the Republic, a new form of government in which those in charge were elected by the people of the State. It was known as SPQR, *Senatores Populusque Romanum*, the Senate and People of Rome. By the time **Julius Caesar** rose to power, Rome had been a Republic for over 400 years and had acquired a vast empire.

The Republic was not, however, a democracy as we understand it today. The Senate was a group of men who debated public issues, made decisions and governed Rome and its Empire. It was dominated by the Patricians, aristocratic families which had provided the lawyers, administrators and generals for many generations. Representatives of the Plebians, the citizens of Rome, were a tiny minority – only five out of 375 Senators.

Power might not lie with only one man, as in the old days of Tarquin, but it still didn't extend much beyond a tight ruling class.

Julius Caesar had the knack of appealing to the people and attracting popular support amongst those who resented the power of the Senate. He was known to be hugely rich as well as a supreme conqueror who had added to the territory and wealth of the Empire.

The opening of the play refers to another general, Pompey, who had been Caesar's rival for power and popularity. Their conflict had plunged Rome into civil war until Pompey had been defeated in battle and killed.

At times of unrest in Rome a dictator was elected to take control and restore order swiftly. He would

The symbol SPQR summed up the idea of the Republic: Senators Popu Romanum, meaning, The Senate and People of Rome.

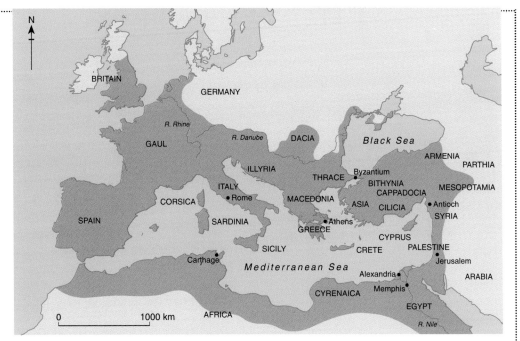

The extent of the Roman Empire at the time of Julius Caesar.

then retire and allow the Senate to resume government. Caesar was elected Dictator in the aftermath of the Civil War but he then went against the accepted order of things and had himself declared Dictator for Life. This was in conflict with the idea of the Republic.

A piece of ancient graffiti sums up these changes. It is a verse written on the statue of Lucius Brutus. He was the man who led the opposition to Tarquin, was the founder of the Republic and its first elected Consul (leader).

' Brutus was elected Consul
When he sent the Kings away
Caesar sent the Consuls packing
Caesar is our King today '

In the play there are references to the fact that **Marcus Brutus** was probably descended from this earlier Brutus so has a family tradition of republicanism and hatred of tyranny.

A laurel wreath was given to the general who was victorious in battle. Julius Caesar often returned to Rome in triumph, wearing a laurel wreath.

THE DEBATE

Shakespeare explores the motivation of those Senators who are so alarmed at Caesar's thirst for power that they plot to kill him. It is perhaps the most famous political assassination of all time. It raises the fundamental question of whether such a killing is ever justifiable: can the aims of the conspirators justify the deed, does the end justify the means? This question is one which had as much significance for the members of Shakespeare's first audience as it has for us in the twentieth century.

It is not surprising that Londoners at The Globe Theatre in 1599 should have found *Julius Caesar* so gripping. At that time London was full of political tension and speculation. The Queen was 66 years old, unmarried and childless. Her long reign had been disturbed by foreign aggression and also by several plots against her life. Some of these sprang from the desire to see a Catholic on the throne of England once again and the Catholic plotters may well have thought that they, like Brutus, had the highest motives.

Elizabeth's chief minister was also her spy master and had informers in every area of public life, even in the theatre. Conspiracy, plots and counter plots were a fact of life in Elizabethan England.

In the twentieth century there has been a plot remarkably similar to the one against **Julius Caesar**. During the Second World War a group of Germans plotted to kill Hitler whom they saw as a tyrant. The group of conspirators included several Christians who had to

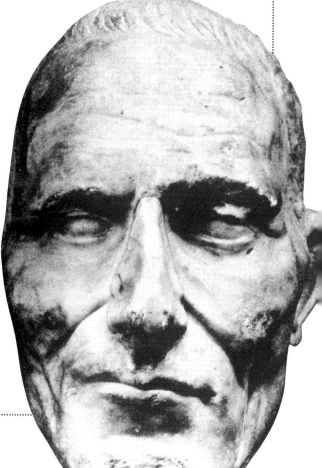

Julius Caesar's death mask.

wrestle with their consciences: tyranny on a large scale, like Hitler's treatment of the Jews, was undoubtedly wrong but the Christians' morality also said it was wrong to kill. They concluded that the end justified the means: their most important aim was to stop Hitler's violence, which meant killing him. They, like Brutus in *Julius Caesar*, came to a moral conclusion that *tyrannicide* – killing a tyrant – was justifiable in some circumstances. There were several assassination attempts against Hitler which didn't get very far, ending in the July Plot of 1944 which also failed.

Julius Caesar becomes, at the end, a political as well as a personal tragedy. Brutus, 'the noblest Roman of them all', joined the conspiracy because of his passionate concern for the well-being of all the people of Rome and his hatred of tyranny. Defeated in battle, he takes the only honourable way out for a Roman of that time – he commits suicide by falling on his own sword. The conspirators fail utterly and power is left in the hands of Caesar's supporters. This raises another question. Is the Republican ideal always doomed to fail?

The question of Julius Caesar's character also provokes different views. Does his popularity explain or even excuse his drive to power?

Does he have the good of the people at heart or is he only selfishly ambitious?

The play therefore asks fundamental questions about government, leadership and democracy.
- What makes a good leader?
- How far can government be shared, both amongst a ruling group and by all citizens?
- What checks are needed to prevent one leader becoming a dictator?

Audiences, actors and students have been rediscovering *Julius Caesar* in each generation for 400 years, which suggests that it is rich in ideas and insight. It does not pretend that there are simple answers to these great political issues.

The debate continues.

A Roman coin commemorating the death of Caesar in 44BC.

THE CHARACTERS

The political debate is presented to the audience through the characters, their thoughts and feelings. It is a play of strong human emotion as well as of ideas.

Julius Caesar has become the most powerful man in the Roman Empire, king in all but name.

Calphurnia is his wife. They have no children.

Marcus Brutus is a leading member of the Senate, the governing body of Rome. Brutus is highly respected as a wise and honourable man.

Portia is Brutus's wife.

Caius Cassius, also a Senator, is a friend of Brutus. He is the ringleader in the plot against Caesar's life.

Casca is another Senator who joins the plot. He is a cool customer and shrewd observer of other people's behaviour.

Trebonius is another conspirator. He gets Mark Antony out of the way before they kill Caesar.

Decius Brutus takes on the vital role of persuading Caesar to go to the Senate House as planned on the Ides of March (15 March), the day set for the assassination. He argues against the effect of Calphurnia's dream, by flattering Caesar.

Metellus Cimber is a conspirator whose brother has been banished from Rome by Caesar.

Cinna is another conspirator.

Caius Ligarius is a sick man whose admiration for Brutus gives him the strength to join the conspiracy.

Mark Antony is Caesar's friend and supporter. He turns the people of Rome against the conspirators and defeats Brutus and Cassius at the Battle of Philippi.

Octavius is Caesar's nephew and heir. He comes to Rome after the assassination and joins Antony and Lepidus to fight against the conspirators.

Lepidus is a soldier and admirer of Caesar who joins Antony and Octavius. With the defeat of the conspirators they will rule Rome as a 'triumvirate': 'The Rule of the Three Men'.

Artemidorus is a Roman who tries to warn Caesar against the conspirators.

Cicero, **Publius** and **Popilius Lena** are Senators who are not part of the conspiracy.

Flavius and **Marullus** are Senators who represent the ordinary people of Rome.

Followers of Brutus and Cassius:

Lucilius	**Messala**
Young Cato	**Volumnius**
Titinius	**Varro**
Clitus	**Claudius**
Dardanius	**Pindarus**
Lucius	**Strato**

The **Soothsayer** warns Caesar, 'Beware the Ides of March'.

Cinna the poet is killed by the mob because he has the same name as one of the conspirators.

People of Rome:

A Cobbler	**A Servant of Octavius**
A Servant of Antony	
A Carpenter	**A Servant of Caesar**

Other soldiers and people of Rome

The **Ghost** of Julius Caesar also appears.

Caesar's image was frequently reproduced during his life-time, on coins and in statues such as this one showing him as a heroic leader.

WHAT HAPPENS

CAESAR, THE RETURNING HERO

Julius Caesar has defeated the armies of the sons of Pompey the Great. He is returning to Rome in triumph: he has finally won the war.

Some of the people have collected in the streets to welcome Caesar. They are sent packing by two senators, **Flavius** and **Marullus**, who remind them that they used to support Pompey. Flavius and Marullus decide to take down all the evidence they find of popular support for Caesar, such as decorations on his statue. Already we can see that there are differences of opinion about Caesar.

THE LUPERCAL GAMES

Caesar and his wife **Calphurnia** attend an athletics contest, part of the celebrations of the Feast of Lupercal. **Mark Antony** is with them. He is going to compete in the games. Caesar reminds Calphurnia to stand where Mark Antony can touch her as he runs, believing that this will help her to have children. A **Soothsayer** (who can see into the future) pushes through the crowd and tells Caesar to take care: something will happen on 'the Ides of March' (15 March). But Caesar dismisses him as a dreamer.

Whilst the games are taking place in the distance, **Brutus** and **Cassius** have a private conversation. Cassius reminds Brutus that Caesar was once their equal, one of a group of leaders of Rome, no better as a soldier or a man than Cassius himself. He fears Caesar's popularity. Just then they hear cheers from the Games and Brutus admits that he, too, is afraid that Caesar might be crowned King of Rome. Cassius tries to persuade Brutus to turn his fears into actions.

Caesar and his followers return from the Games. Caesar tells Mark Antony that he does not trust Cassius. Brutus and Cassius ask **Casca**, another Senator, what happened at the Games. Casca tells them that Mark Antony, backed up by the crowd, offered Caesar a crown three times. Caesar refused to accept it but, Casca thinks, very reluctantly.

THE CONSPIRACY

Cassius takes the lead in forming a group of Senators who are opposed to Caesar. They think he has become king in all but name, and so is a danger to the republican government. Cassius and his fellow conspirators meet at night during a terrible storm. For Cassius this storm is a sign of the danger Rome is in from Caesar.

The conspirators go to Brutus who agrees that they must kill Caesar. They will assassinate him the next day in the Senate House.

Brutus's wife, **Portia**, asks what is troubling him. Doesn't he think she can keep a secret? Portia tells Brutus that she has given herself a wound in the thigh and kept the pain to herself, as a proof of her strong character. Surely he can treat her as a real wife and not keep his deepest thoughts to himself. Brutus is convinced and promises to tell her about his fears and his plans.

'Wherefore rejoice? What conquest brings he home?' The people of Rome await Caesar, but two senators send them home. They don't like his popularity with the people. Directed by Ron Daniels, for the RSC in 1983.

THE MORNING OF THE IDES OF MARCH

Calphurnia tries to persuade Caesar not to go to the Senate House. She is convinced he is in danger: she dreamed she saw his statue running with blood. At first Caesar dismisses her fears, telling her he never changes his mind, but in the end he gives way and agrees to stay at home.

Decius Brutus, one of the conspirators, now arrives. He manages to change Caesar's mind again by reinterpreting Calphurnia's dream in a way that flatters Caesar. The other conspirators join Decius Brutus and Caesar, and all go to the Senate House together.

THE DEATH OF CAESAR

As Caesar walks by, **Artemidorus** gives him a letter warning him about the conspirators. He begs Caesar to read it but Caesar says he will not deal with personal matters until after public affairs. He ignores the letter.

The conspirators make sure that Mark Antony is in another room, then they turn on Caesar and stab him. The last one to strike a blow is Brutus. As he dies Caesar says:

'Et tu Brute? [You too, Brutus?] – Then fall Caesar.'

The conspirators smear their hands with Caesar's blood as a public sign of what they have done. Now they must go to the Forum, Rome's public meeting place, and explain to the people why they have killed Caesar. They sum it up for themselves in the phrase 'tyranny is dead'; they have given Rome its freedom.

Now Mark Antony comes in and sees the body. He is shocked and perhaps expects to be killed too. Brutus assures him that he is safe, that he will give reasons for the killing, and will even allow Antony to speak at Caesar's funeral. Cassius tries to stop this generous gesture but Brutus overrules him.

CAESAR'S FUNERAL

Caesar's body is displayed in public and Brutus is the first to speak. He tells the people of Rome that Caesar was killed because he had become too ambitious.

Brutus keeps his word and allows Mark Antony to take the platform and speak in praise of Caesar. Antony's speech cleverly turns Brutus's charge that Caesar was ambitious into a sign of the greatness of the dead man. If Caesar was ambitious, then he was ambitious for Rome, and planned to give the people of Rome many good things. So Antony's speech turns the people against the conspirators and their anger at Caesar's death explodes into violence. Brutus and Cassius are forced to escape from Rome but others, such as **Cinna** the poet, are not so lucky and are killed by the mob.

'Most noble brother, you have done me wrong.'
The meeting of Brutus (Rob Edwards) and Cassius
(Jeffrey Kissoon), RSC, 1993, directed by David Thacker.

PREPARING FOR BATTLE

Mark Antony joins forces with **Lepidus**, an experienced soldier and former supporter of Caesar and **Octavius**, Caesar's nephew. They raise an army to fight against Brutus, Cassius and their followers.

Brutus and Cassius quarrel: Brutus accuses Cassius of refusing to send money to help pay the soldiers, Cassius says he is hurt that his friend should have thought so badly of him. It is almost the breaking point between them but they just manage to cling on to their old friendship. Brutus tells Cassius that he has had news of Portia. She had been left behind in Rome and, frantic about her husband's safety, has killed herself.

THE BATTLE AT PHILIPPI

The ghost of Caesar appears to Brutus the night before the final battle. The dead Caesar threatens to haunt Brutus on the battlefield.

The two sets of generals meet for the last time. Antony, Octavius and Lepidus face Cassius and Brutus but there is no chance of a reconciliation. Battle is inevitable. Just before the fighting begins, Brutus and Cassius have a final conversation. They discuss whether or not it would be honourable to commit suicide if they were defeated rather than submit to Antony and Octavius and be led as prisoners through the streets of Rome. Suicide was considered a brave and honourable way for a defeated soldier to die. During the battle which follows, Cassius's troops quickly lose heart and some try to run away. Cassius sends **Titinius** to find out what is happening and Cassius's slave **Pindarus** keeps a look-out. It seems to Pindarus as if Titinius is taken prisoner. When Cassius hears this he falls into despair and, feeling that his useful life is over, commands Pindarus to hold his sword while he falls on it. Reluctantly Pindarus agrees and so Cassius dies.

Tragically Pindarus had misunderstood: Titinius had not been taken prisoner. He comes back with the news that Brutus's soldiers have overthrown Octavius's army only to find that Cassius is dead. Brutus's triumph is short-lived.

Facing the failure of all his hopes, Brutus decides to take his own life. He also asks a servant, **Clitus**, to hold his sword but Clitus refuses, saying he would rather kill himself. Another servant, **Volumnius**, says the same. Finally **Strato** agrees, holding the sword for Brutus to fall on.

Antony and Octavius have won the war and are left to govern Rome. Antony praises the dead Brutus as 'the noblest Roman of them all'. Only Brutus believed that what he did was for the good of Rome, the rest of the conspirators, says Antony, were envious of Caesar.

'You will compel me then to read the will?'
Antony's funeral oration, Act 3; Scene 2.
Owen Teale as Mark Antony in Pimlott's
1991 production.

JULIUS CAESAR
ON STAGE

*J*ulius Caesar, perhaps more than any other of Shakespeare's plays, has been seen in a new way by each generation of actors who have discovered it. This view of a play is called the 'interpretation' – the way actors understand its ideas and meaning and make that clear to their audience. Any interpretation which holds the audience's interest has to grow from the text – the words on the page – not contradict it. Even so, performances can differ considerably from each other.

A lavish stage setting of the assassination scene in Herbert Beerbohm Tree's production at Her Majesty's Theatre in London 1898.

One of the main differences between performances is in the balance between the main characters. Actors have always asked themselves which is the main part in the play, **Brutus** or **Mark Antony**. How important is **Caesar** himself? Occasionally a leading actor has chosen **Cassius** as the most interesting person. These choices will affect what the audiences see, and how they understand the play.

Julius Caesar grew in popularity during the nineteenth century. Many productions made Brutus the hero – wise, unselfish, courageous, suffering nobly for what he believed. With this in mind, some actors 'tidied up' Brutus' death scene: their versions had him dying alone, and often a new speech was written for him which referred to his 'beloved country'.

THE ACTOR-MANAGERS TAKE THE STAGE

In the nineteenth century the actor-manager became the leading figure in the theatre. He combined playing major roles with the job of running the organization and finances of the company. Perhaps the equivalents today are those film actors who also have a financial stake in their projects and take charge of most elements of organizing and making the film. Victorian actor-managers were tremendously energetic, dominating personalities for whom playing the lead was not enough;

they had to create the whole stage picture too.

A production staged at Covent Garden in London in 1812 by the actor-manager John Philip Kemble tried to idealize Mark Antony as well as Brutus. Any part of Shakespeare's text which suggested that Antony was cunning or ruthless was cut out. Kemble filled his stage with a large crowd who were present for a lot of the play but rarely moved. For us this might sound dull but Kemble's productions were very popular at the time, described by one member of his audience as 'animated paintings'. They began a taste for grand spectacle in productions of *Julius Caesar*.

At the end of the century London had another smash hit in a production which ran for the unusually long period of five months and made a profit of £11,000. Beerbohm Tree, the actor-manager, played Mark Antony. Like Kemble he enjoyed making stage pictures but, unlike Kemble, his pictures moved and came to life. He tried to find out what ancient Rome was like and to show it on stage. Above all he liked big effects, full of realistic detail. Members of the crowd all had their own tasks and actions. This was a step forward in style of performance and appealed to audiences at the time as much more interesting than the old grand spectacle.

DIRECTORS' PERSPECTIVES

I n this century the actor-manager has often been replaced by a director. The director is responsible for all aspects of the production and for the actors' performances. His or her view of the play guides the work of everyone else involved and aims to give the production a coherent style and meaning. Unlike the actor-manager the director does not act but guides the rehearsals and performances, keeping a critical eye on their development.

Many directors begin by talking to the designer about the play. They need to agree on how the ideas, the story and the atmosphere can be communicated in visual terms. This is achieved through the spaces and setting created on stage and through other elements like lighting, costume, style of furniture and stage objects. One of the major decisions which the director and designer have to make with *Julius Caesar* is whether it should be set in ancient Rome. The actor-managers usually wanted to be historically accurate but many directors have made other choices.

For example, in 1937 Orson Welles gave New York theatre-goers a completely fresh slant on the political meaning of *Julius Caesar*. He subtitled it *Death of a Dictator* and used modern dress and staging style to show parallels with the rise of Fascism in Europe. This bold,

Orson Welles' production in New York in 1937 used modern dress to bring home the relevance of the political debate in *Julius Caesar* at the time when Hitler was coming to power and Fascism was sweeping Europe.

The death of Brutus, Act 5 Scene 5 in Glen Byam Shaw's production in 1957 which stressed the qualities of Caesar as a great leader. This view of him was echoed in a later production at the National Theatre in 1977.

rushed period of rehearsal, a director will usually work with actors in great detail, exploring the layers of meaning in Shakespeare's language. Modern audiences of this play are interested in why characters do what they do, as well as in ideas and stage pictures.

The director leads the actor to explore and make sense of his or her character's inner life of ambition, fear or disappointment. S/he then has to work out how to express these inner feelings in the way s/he speaks Shakespeare's language. For example, the emphasis which the actor playing **Mark Antony** gives to his repeated line,

> **'Yet Brutus says he was ambitious**
> **And Brutus is an honourable man'**

tells us a lot about his character. Does he sound bitter, sarcastic, angry, puzzled, full of grief?

If Orson Welles saw **Caesar** as a dictator who had to die, other directors have explored other possibilities. A National Theatre production in London in 1977, directed by John Schlesinger, was unusual in the emphasis it placed on Caesar himself as a hero in decline, an extraordinary man who had once commanded most of the known world. This Caesar had a strength which dominated the personalities of everyone around him.

strong direction stressed 'the issues of political violence and the moral duty of the individual in the face of tyranny'. Modern dress has frequently been used to emphasize the continuing relevance of the play.

In *Julius Caesar* the director also has important choices to explore with the actors. Unlike the actor-manager's often superficial and

RSC PRODUCTIONS

Directors at the Royal Shakespeare Company have explored some interesting alternative settings to ancient Rome.

In 1991 Steven Pimlott emphasized the theatrical nature of politics, the sense in which a politician is 'acting' for so much of his or her public life. He and his designer created a stage setting with huge side pillars. This reminded the audience of Rome but also made a frame for the scenes which were played out within them, rather like the frame of a painting. They also used several platforms within the stage space to make all the set speeches more theatrical in style of presentation.

This production used the two strongly contrasting colours of red and blue: the colours of Republican and Imperial Rome, and in themselves a dramatic way of expressing conflict. The actors' costumes were based on the view of ancient Rome favoured by painters of the Renaissance (before and during Shakespeare's time).

Robert Stephens as Caesar in Steven Pimlott's production for the RSC, 1991. The costumes and setting reminded the audience of Renaissance paintings of ancient Rome.

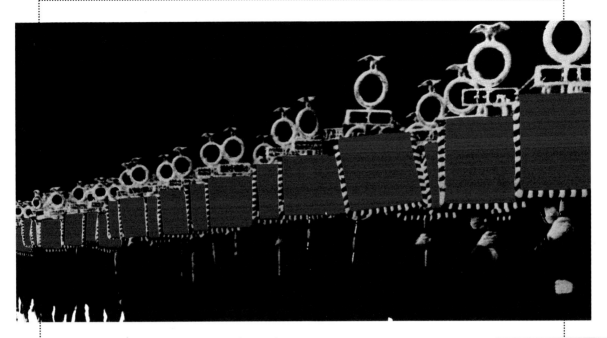

Grand processions showed the military power of Caesar in this production at Stratford 1972 directed by Trevor Nunn.

There were men in togas but also some in short tunics. One of the effects of the various design elements was to make the stage look like a Renaissance painting come to life. This stressed the fact that the play was of its own time, the late sixteenth century, as well as about the life and death of Caesar 1500 years before.

In 1972 the Director of the RSC, Trevor Nunn, staged *Julius Caesar* as part of a cycle of Shakespeare's Roman plays. This was a very unusual and interesting way of thinking about the big political questions raised by the plays. The director included grand processions to suggest the overbearing power of the ruling class, particularly of **Caesar** himself. The People obviously had no chance of voicing their opinions but they were present on stage, in a good sized crowd, always on the receiving end of the Senators' anger or attempts to control their feelings.

The next production, directed by Terry Hands in 1987, got rid of the crowd almost entirely. Atmosphere was created by strong blood-red lighting beamed on to stark brick walls. This performance focused very closely on the group of conspirators and particularly on the differences between **Cassius** and **Brutus**. **Mark Antony** had the difficult task of playing his great funeral speech to a near empty stage with the response of the People merely a tape-recorded sound track.

JULIUS CAESAR FOR THE 1990s

Another notable RSC production of *Julius Caesar* was directed by David Thacker in 1993. This production was in modern dress, including contemporary army uniform. It was set, unusually, in an arena space. About two thirds of the audience sat in steeply raked seats looking down on to an empty circular acting area – a ring with a red carpet on the floor. It was like being at the circus or some sporting contest. The rest of the audience came into the acting arena with the actors at the start of the performance and stayed throughout. They could stand or sit and move around the space as they wished. The actors performed amongst the promenaders (the standing audience) so that the entire cycle of events took place within a crowd.

David Thacker and his designer had been impressed by the recent media coverage of political events and fighting in Eastern Europe. Great political changes were seen to happen always within the mass of people. Television and newspapers showed people in cities queuing for food or fleeing for their lives or being caught up in battles which they didn't cause. This production, therefore, with the audience as crowd caught up in the action and witnessing everything at close quarters, focused attention on our modern world.

Barry Lynch as Mark Antony mourning the death of Caesar played by David Sumner in David Thacker's arena production for the RSC in 1993. The audience was intimately involved in the action witnessing the reality of political conflict in close-up.

DIFFERENT DIRECTORS: DIFFERENT INTERPRETATIONS

The differences in directors' perspectives on *Julius Caesar* show that there is no one simple way of understanding the play. The characters are complex and the relationships which drive the action forward can be seen in several ways. The director also makes choices about the broad sweep of ideas in the play. He or she can stress the particular political attitude which will mean most to the audience at that particular time.

Shakespeare wrote 400 years ago but we are still exploring and finding new meanings in his work, and he remains the most frequently performed playwright.

Army uniforms from several different countries were used in this modern dress production staged in the round. RSC 1993, director, David Thacker.

Actors' Perspectives

Julius Caesar

Frank Benson was one of the great actor-managers of the nineteenth century who travelled throughout Britain playing Shakespeare with his company of actors. He achieved success in more than one of the leading roles in *Julius Caesar*. He found nobility and traces of greatness in **Caesar** and enjoyed playing the role. He was also admired for the passionate conviction of his **Antony**. Actors like Frank Benson made a point of looking for high ideals in all the main characters but this now seems a rather old-fashioned attitude.

More recent productions have emphasized the corrupting effects of power on Caesar and the danger of tyranny. In 1987 the actor David Waller showed a Caesar full of vanity, in love with his own popularity, and pompous. Robert Stephens created a more sinister figure in the RSC production of 1991: ever smiling, with a chilling sense of danger about him so that we believed he could be capable of any kind of cruelty.

In 1993 David Sumner played Julius Caesar for the RSC. In preparing to play the role he read not only Plutarch but also Suetonius, another contemporary historical biographer. Their pictures of Caesar's character reinforced Sumner's feeling that Shakespeare's Caesar was attracted by risk and, as leader of a vast empire, played with high stakes. In the scene where the conspirators come to fetch Caesar and escort him to the Senate, David Sumner often played Caesar as if he half suspected danger but gambled on being able to avoid it. He was a glamorous figure, a media star who went walk-about in the crowds and was always introduced on public occasions by a stirring fanfare.

David Sumner playing Julius Caesar in the 1993 RSC production.

Marlon Brando played Mark Antony as young, athletic and passionate in the very successful MGM film.

Actors have to make sense of Antony in the light of this final speech. The big questions facing them are about the degree to which he is cunning and manipulative.

Marlon Brando's good-looking young athlete in the MGM film perhaps gave a model for an Antony who starts as a play-boy and who grows up politically during the events. Owen Teale gave a performance at Stratford in 1991 which was along these lines. His Antony was full of vitality and enthusiasm in the early scene before the Lupercal Games and was apparently deeply shocked and moved by the death.

MARK ANTONY

Brutus is opposed in the play by Mark Antony. They are the two who speak to the people at Caesar's funeral and also put opposing views of the dead man to the citizens. They then become enemies. At the end of the play, on the battlefield at Philippi, Antony acknowledges Brutus's virtue in a generous tribute:

> **'This was the noblest Roman of them all;**
> **All the conspirators, save only he**
> **Did what they did in envy of great Caesar.'**

The next major production, again at Stratford, in 1993, had a very compelling Antony played by Barry Lynch. He was a manipulator right from the start. In the scene immediately following the assassination, when Antony first saw the body of Caesar surrounded by all the conspirators, he took their hands one by one, saying it was a sign of friendship despite what they had done. Barry Lynch succeeded in giving this repeated action a charge of ritualized menace. The audience felt that Antony was privately pledging himself to take revenge on all the men whose bloody hands he took.

CASSIUS

This character has been reclaimed by actors this century. Most nineteenth-century actors played him as a rather one-dimensional man governed by irrational feelings, envy and quick temper. He was very much in contrast to the noble Brutus.

Sir John Gielgud played **Cassius** in a famous production at Stratford in 1951 and brought out the complexity of the man. His Cassius was jealous of others' success and frustrated because he had a strong sense of his own ability. In this performance the audience could believe that all the leading Senators were men of great experience who, together, had ruled the world. It was understandable that one of them should feel slighted when Caesar emerged as leader.

After playing Cassius on stage Gielgud played the same part in 1952 for MGM in Hollywood. This film of *Julius Caesar* was one of the most successful cinema versions of a Shakespeare play. Gielgud appreciated the camera's ability to come in close for scenes showing intimate, private emotions and to pan out for the busy public scenes. This cinematic quality was a real advantage in presenting the play. The MGM film also featured Marlon Brando as an athletic, heroic Mark Antony (see page 27). Young and passionate, he was in direct contrast to the worldly-wise Cassius.

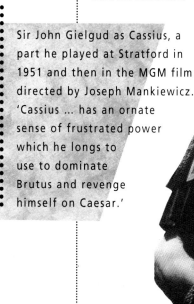

Sir John Gielgud as Cassius, a part he played at Stratford in 1951 and then in the MGM film directed by Joseph Mankiewicz. 'Cassius ... has an ornate sense of frustrated power which he longs to use to dominate Brutus and revenge himself on Caesar.'

In the 1993 RSC production of *Julius Caesar* (see page 24) Cassius was played by Rob Edwards. His Cassius was highly intelligent, realistic about politics, brave and unselfishly committed to his cause. He cared deeply for his friendship with Brutus. The tragedy of Cassius's life and death was very strong in this performance.

Rob Edwards portrayed Cassius as a true revolutionary who believed that men, not fate or 'the Gods', rule their own lives. Cassius's famous comment is the key to his philosophy:

> **'The fault, dear Brutus, is not in our stars,**
> **But in ourselves, that we are underlings.'**

This Cassius was driven by passionate anger at the destruction of Rome's democratic principles. He was obviously quite prepared to die if the plot against Caesar were to go wrong. Rob Edwards summed him up:

> **'Revolution or death – the credo of the freedom fighter.'**

His performance was also acutely aware of Cassius's emotions. He was a man looking for love, a man who desperately needed Brutus's friendship.

Rob Edwards played Cassius for the RSC in 1993. 'Revolution or death – the credo of the freedom fighter.' He was revolutionary in public and in need of Brutus' love and respect in private.

BRUTUS

As Cassius has become a more interesting role for modern actors to play, Brutus has become harder. We recognize Cassius's complexity and mixed motives, he is like us. Brutus, the man of honour but perhaps politically naïve, seems more remote.

Many productions in the nineteenth century presented the play as the tragedy of Brutus and this interpretation was particularly popular in Europe. Republicanism was an idea which had taken root following the French Revolution of 1789 and the founding of the French Republic. So in many European countries, despite bitter clashes between political radicals and traditionalists, the ideal of democratic republicanism survived. For such thinkers, whether in the theatres or universities, Brutus was a great model of the noble leader who stood up against tyranny and tried to give his country freedom.

It is interesting that a much admired modern production of *Julius Caesar*, directed by Peter Stein in Salzburg in 1992, continued this view of the play. Brutus, played by

Roger Allam as Brutus in Terry Hands' production for the RSC in 1988; a sensitive idealist.

Thomas Holtzmann, was a highly intelligent, sensitive man apalled by the bloody reality of what he and the conspirators had to do. He seemed almost to welcome the suffering and death which came afterwards. This performance showed Brutus as a man caught in a moral trap. The actor emphasized Brutus' suffering in agonizing over whether or not to join the plot. The act of killing was therefore seen as the lesser of two evils – an awesome duty for which a price had to be paid.

Recent productions in England have presented Brutus less as super man, but more as struggling human being. In a Stratford production in 1972 John Wood even showed the failings of such a thoughtful man: always agonizing over his actions, incapable of coming to a strong decision about what was politically necessary. One theatre critic summed up this Brutus as a 'bone-headed liberal'.

In 1987 Roger Allam created a Brutus who was a suffering man of honour, hating the necessity of acting dishonourably but who nevertheless found the moral courage to do so. He also emphasized Brutus' pain at the death of Portia by making Brutus burn the letter which gave him the news of Portia's death. From that moment on he was a man in despair who knew that his end was in sight.

John Wood played Brutus in Trevor Nunn's 1972 production which staged *Julius Caesar* as part of a cycle of all Shakespeare's Roman plays.

INDEX